I0468592

How To Get
The Job You Want

Shonda Miles

For more information on Shonda Miles, go to www.shondamiles.com. Shonda Miles offers a range of Products and Services including Multiple Streams of Income-how to make money while you sleep and How to make an extra $100,000 this year.

Other books by Author

10 Ways to Write an Ebook every 10 days

101 Success Questions

Remote Medical Coding Jobs

What I wish I knew before starting a business

How to Love Your Spouse again

How to Double Your Income in 12 Months or less

50 Tips to Jumpstart Your Success

50 Streams of Income

18 Ways to Break into Coding

How to get the Job You want

21 Ways to Start a Marriage off Right

21 Ways to Make a Blended Family Work

How to get clients for your business

Keys to Success

Marty learns to swim

I am

I am for girls

I am for boys

I am for teens

How to create audio products

Table of Contents

Introduction

I wanted to write this book because I watched as so many people struggled to get the job they wanted. Most people make the same common mistakes. I spent months studying interview skills, job search and how to get the job I wanted. During my research I came across certain key tips over and over again. I also learned a ton from my own experience.

Job Search is a challenge as it is. It is important to follow the rules of Job Search. Job Search doesn't have to be hard. There are certain things you can do to increase your chances of getting the job you want.

The problem most people have is not knowing what they want. If all you want is a job then this will work for you quicker than doing nothing. If you want a great job, then this will certainly help you in your job search.

Job Search requires a commitment to the search process. Dedicate adequate time to look for a job.

Why don't you imagine the best? Picture yourself succeeding.

"Infinite money potentially awaits each of us who apply the principles of acquiring it.

You can decide to become wealthy or abundant now and the Universe will cheerfully provide. Opportunities and blessings come to individuals who embrace an abundance attitude. Others everywhere have created abundance, so can you.

Abundant thinking multiples, magnetizes and magnifies whatever is focused upon.

Sharing always creates more.

To "out – picture "abundance we first must successfully and repetitively "in picture" a mental state of abundance. Why? Because our state of mind creates our state of results.

Give, and it will be given to you. Give your time, your approval, your smile, your advice, your wisdom, your compliments, your sense of humor, your talent, your attention, your encouragement, your love."

"Getting your act together is the final key to manifesting what you want your life.

Feed your dreams, stave your doubts

* Control your thinking and you control your results.

* As you ask yourself better questions, your results will vastly improve."

The only time you are actually growing is when you are uncomfortable.

"If you want to improve your income and your status in life, you must carefully examine the relationships in your life and see how the influence of others is affecting you." – Tom Corson Knowles.

Research

Take out a piece of paper. Make a list of companies you want to work for.

Research the company that you want to work for. You can Google the company. Look for open positions.

What jobs do they have available to you? Are you interested in any of them?

Look the company up on LinkedIn. What names come up? What supervisors name come up? What departments are they over? Take notes. Look at their experience. What skills do they have? What jobs have they had? Which ones might be over a job you are interested in doing. See what groups or associations they are apart of. Start networking with them.

Review

Review the requirements of the job. When you're looking at the requirements of a job, you want to match up the requirements of the job with your skills and past experiences.

What are the key skills most of the jobs you want require?

Cover Letters

Always write a cover letter for any job you are applying to. Keep Cover Letter to one page. This is one of the most neglected things by most job applicants. This is important as it will make you stand out. It takes time but it's super easy.

What you want to do is pull from the requirements of the job and match up with your experience so the employer knows that you have this experience.

Also when you're reviewing the requirements of a job you want to pull those key words out and put them in your resume, whether it's under your skills section or qualifications section. You want to pull those key words out and put them in your resume. Especially in your resume, but also on your cover letter as well. Only use the ones applicable to your job experience.

The reason why it's so important to pull the key words from the job requirements and put into your resume is because most applications now are done electronically.

Part of the reason why is because technology is changing so fast. It's also because the number of applicants that are applying for jobs used to be a dozen or so, now it could be in the hundreds.

The way employers rule you out is by using these keywords. They have a filter that says, "These key words don't show up in this person's resume, and then you are weeded out." Even though you might be qualified to do the job. You want to make sure that you're using the key words pulled directly from the job description or job posting.

1234 ABC Street   (123) 456-7890

Dream Job, USA professionalemail@yahoo.com 45678

October 21, 2013

Name of person resume is going to if known

His or her title

Name of company

Address

City, State Zip

To Whom It May Concern:

My 15 plus years' experience in Medical Billing, Coding, and Auditing makes me a great candidate for the Remote coding position.

My qualifications include:

- Certified Coding Specialist (CCS) Keywords employer is looking for

- 4 years' experience as Auditor

- 13 years coding Physician Services

- ICD-10 training

- 1995 and 1997 guidelines experience

- 8 years coding for a teaching hospital

- Executive Masters of Business Administration

- 10 years Management Experience, Previous experience as CEO/President

- Taught classes at Remington College in Professional Development, Medical Coding, Medical Billing, Anatomy and Physiology

- Teach Medical Coding and Billing at Online School

I am committed to the coding field, and I am focused on accuracy. I look forward to speaking with you about this opportunity.

Thank you for your time and consideration.

Sincerely,

Marmeshonda (Shonda) Miles, MBA, CCS, CCS-P, CPC
(Any Certifications if applicable, higher degrees)

Enclosure: Resume

Resume

Keep Resume to 2 pages or less. Use a different resume for each job you apply for making subtle tweaks as needed. Be sure to save under that Job titles. Companies sometimes call the same job something different based on employer. Check your resume for spelling and grammatical errors. This is a big no-no, and this happens more frequently than not. Maybe you've looked at your resume so many times, maybe you need a fresh set of eyes on it. Of course, Microsoft Word has tried to do their best to offer the red and green squiggly lines for spelling and grammatical errors, but you might just get a fresh set of eyes and get someone else to look at it for you.

Take off work older than 10 years or older unless you have been with your current employer longer than 10 years. In other words, you want at least 2 previous jobs besides where you are currently if applicable. You don't won't to use jobs you had in high school if you are in your 30s.

When you have jobs on your resume that you've done in the past, you want to make sure that you have added the -ed indicating that they were in the past. When you look at your resume you know, for example, if I filed last year, then I'd do "filed" with an -ed versus "file", because file will indicate that I'm doing it presently.

Google Resumes for the Job you are searching for and your industry as well.

Make sure your email is a professional one.

Core Competencies should be keywords taken directly from the Job description.

Always spell check all documents.

Don't include months on your resume especially if you are trying to cover up short periods of time.

Your Name, MBA, CCS, CCS-P, CPC

1234 Going Places Dr   (123) 456-7809

Going Places, USA 12345   professionalemail@yahoo.com

HIM CHART REVIEW CONSULTANT

EDUCATION

Certified Coding Specialist   2012
(CCS)

AHIMA

Certified Coding Specialist-   2012
Physician (CCS-P)

AHIMA

Certified Professional Coder   2009
(CPC)

American Academy of Professional Coders (AAPC)

Executive Masters of Business Administration

| Colorado Technical University, Colorado Springs, CO | 2007 |

Bachelor of Science, Business Administration

| Colorado Technical University, Colorado Springs, CO | 2006 |

Magna Cum Laude GPA 3.7

Medical Office Specialist

| American School of Business | 2000 |

CORE COMPETENCIES Your Industry Keywords that match your experience

ASC/SDS/OBS/ED	MS-DRG
APC	ICD-10 PCS
RAC/CERT	Auditing
EPIC/Centricity	Intelicode Pro
Citrix/NextGen	3M/Encoder Pro
IDX	Interventional Radiology
Home Health/Nursing Home	Clinical Documentation Improv

POAs/HACs	MPFS/RVU's
Meditech	Level 1 Trauma
Clintrac	PowerChart
Canopy	ChartOne/ewebhealth
HDM/Citrix	TruCode
VPNs	Sovera
Sunrise	Affinity
Quantim	ICD-10 CM

PROFESSIONAL EXPERIENCE

Kingsley Rose   2015-present

REMOTE CODER/AUDITOR

- Analyzed and interpreted inpatient, medical records to ensure complete and accurate coding based on ICD-9 Coding Guidelines and UHDDS

- Coded all pertinent comorbid and complications as well as invasive procedures

- Validated discharge disposition code assignment

- Coded all diagnostic and operative information from the medical record using ICD-9-CM, CPT and HCPCS coding classification systems

Professional Development Training Company-Shreveport, LA   2003-2007

(Consulting Company)

MANAGEMENT CONSULTANT

- Assisted small businesses with services from business plan development, to marketing and strategic decision making

- Analyzed financial performance of small businesses

PREVIOUS EXPERIENCE

Willis Knighton Health System
  2001-2003

(250 bed, nonprofit)

INPATIENT/OUTPATIENT MEDICAL CODER

- Codes all pertinent comorbid and complications as well as invasive procedures

- Responsible for assigning ICD-9, CPT-4 codes to obtain accurate DRG or APC assignment for proper reimbursement and data collection
- Assign POA (Present on Admission) indicators per official guidelines
- Validate discharge disposition code assignment

Professional Associations

AHIMA	2012-present
ACIDS	2012-present
AAPC	2009-present

Thank You Letters

Send a thank-you letter to all the interviewers. If it's multi-panel or a panel of interviewers, ask for a business card. Sometimes they have them on their desk or you could ask for the correct spelling of their name.

You could write it down at the beginning of the interview or even at the end of the interview. Sometimes you can get it from the gatekeeper or the receptionist.

You want to make sure you get the correct spelling of their name, their position and the address of the company so that you could send a thank-you letter. You want to stand out to the employer.

Make sure you send a thank-you letter and use a cover letter, it will be extremely helpful since most people don't take the time to do it. Try to send a Thank You Letter the day of the interview or the next day.

It could keep you from getting a job even if you're qualified. Always thank the interviewer as you're leaving, shake hands with them again. I would say, "Nice to meet you. It was nice to meet you." You always want to have a set of questions to ask the interviewer. You can make a list of, seven to ten questions. If you only have two or three, then the employer answers those questions during the interview then you're left with nothing to ask the interviewer. You want to make sure you have seven to ten good questions, and then at the end you want to ask them, "What is the next step?" Or "What can I tell you that I haven't already to highlighted my experience?" If you don't ask questions, it could seem as if you are not really interested in the job.

In your thank-you letter I would clear up anything that maybe you forgot to say or that you weren't clear about. If you have to take a personality test either before or after the interview, you just want to be careful. You always want to answer questions with what you know you should do. Remember, employers want honest people who look out for the company and can solve problems on their own.

Sample Thank You Letter

Take out parts that are not appropriate. Be sure that everything is spelled correctly. If you are not sure, ask. This will set you apart from other applicants.

Your street address
Your City, State and Zip Code

Phone Number

Your email address

Today's Date

Interviewer Name John Doe
Job Title
Name of the Employer
ABC Street Address
City, State and Zip Code

Dear *Mr./Ms. Last Name:*

Thank you for the opportunity to interview for the position of *XYZ today, if appropriate].* I enjoyed speaking with you, meeting other members of the staff, and the opportunity to learn more about this position. I am very interested in this position and the opportunity to join your team.

This paragraph is where you will sell yourself. You will clear up anything that needs to cleared up or clarified. You can add anything you think might be helpful. This job seems like a good match between my skills and experience and the requirements of this job. As we discussed, you need someone with strong *[whatever]* skills, and I have extensive experience with *[whatever technology or tool that is important to the job and that you have experience using].* In addition, in my current *[or former]* job as *[names or* *type of employer in your past]* has provided the opportunity to polish my skills in *[whatever]* and *[whatever]* needed for your *[job title]* position.

Again, thank you for considering me for this wonderful opportunity. Please let me know if you have any questions or concerns. I look forward to hearing from you *whenever they said they would be in touch.* I hope to join your staff soon.

Best regards,

Your Name
Your Phone number

Google

If you know ahead of time who you're going to be interviewed by, you can Google that person. Look them up on LinkedIn. See what you can find out about them. It might help you with some tips on how to break the ice and build rapport.

Google your name

Google your name. You would go to google.com and type your name into the search box and see what comes up under your name. Chances are there's a bunch of people with your same name. But what you want to do is look for things that might come up under your name.

Look for things that could hurt you in an interview. Maybe your Facebook page, maybe things that are not private that should be private, or anything negative.

You want to know it before your potential employer knows it. More than likely somebody in HR will Google your name. They will look you up on LinkedIn as well.

They will check you out on Facebook. You want to make sure all these things are in order. Be sure that you're not using profanity, that you're not partying, that you're not drinking on social media. You want to look like a professional on these websites.

Know how

Go to the company's website, and just find out as much information about the company as you can. Look at the press releases and any history. This will help you in the interview process, because most interviewers will ask, "What do you know about the company?" Or "Why do you want to work for us?" With this information you're able to pull from what you've learned on the website and answer these questions.

Know how to answer the top twenty interview questions. This is so important. Most interviewers, they use the same standard questions. If you know the answers to the top twenty questions, this will drastically help you.

Practice how to answer them. You don't want to be too stiff. You should have your key points wrote down. You want to know how to emphasize them.

This will help you in the interview. It's always amazing to me how many people stumble through questions they know they are going to be asked during the interview. Reduce this stress, practice ahead of time. Don't plan on winging it.

It's when you don't take the time to write down the twenty questions, that really gets you in trouble.

The way I see it is, if you have these twenty questions wrote down, any other question that they ask you outside of these twenty, you could pull from the answers to these twenty questions to help you with the interview process, instead of using the notorious, "Uh, uh ... "

Make sure your answers are sharp and clear.

We know the typical ones are, "Tell me about yourself." You want to make sure that you highlight key experiences that would be pertinent to the job that you're applying for. The next one is strengths. What are your strengths?

Of course the infamous, "Tell me about yourself" is a very important question that you need to have a good solid answer telling the interviewer about yourself.

The person that's interviewing you will definitely ask you in some shape or form your strengths, your weaknesses, and of course we don't want to look bad to the interviewer.

We all have weaknesses. You want to use a weakness that is not pertinent to the job that you're applying for.

You will get asked, "Why should we hire you?" "What do you know about our company?"

"Tell me about a time when you went over and beyond."

"Tell me about a time when you and your boss disagreed." These are situational interview questions, but chances are you will be asked something like this.

"Tell me about a time when your boss told you to do something that you didn't want to do, or that you didn't feel was right."

When you get the interview you want to exude self-confidence. I like what Brian Tracy says, "I like myself. I like myself. I like myself." To increase your self-confidence, and I totally believe this- you should go in standing up straight, your back upright, sit up straight, smile. You're exhibiting self-confidence. You want to give a firm handshake.

You want to be confident in the interview. You want to show that you are qualified to do this job. You are the best person for this job and you want that to show during the interview. They would be making a mistake if they didn't hire you.

Think positive about the interview. Visualize yourself doing well in the interview. See yourself getting the job. Picture yourself coming into the job.

Something else you want to keep in mind is all employers want to know you are dependable, a leader, a problem-solver, team player, and that you work with little or no supervision. When you're answering your interview questions you want to make sure that you have in some way, have indicated that you're dependable, a leader, solve problems, a team player, and that you work well with little or no supervision.

If you go to the interview and you don't get the job, what you want to do is call back and ask them was there something that you could've done better? Ask for some feedback? Then use that information for the next interview to get better.

You want to make sure that you're smiling during the interview process, you want to be sitting up straight in your chair. You want to make sure that you give a firm handshake to the interviewer, everyone that you're being interviewed by.

Appearance

Dress to impress. You want to make sure that your appearance is based on the job. Always try to dress up at least a notch for the job. I believe that men should always wear ties no matter what job that they're applying for. It will make you stand out among your competition. If you have tattoos or extra piercings, try to cover them up. As for extra piercings I would take out. You really want to be careful what you're wearing, try to dress conservatively.

Make sure that you arrive early for the interview. I cannot tell you how many times I have found myself stuck in traffic, behind a train, and all these different things. Plan to arrive early. Leave home a little bit early. What I recommend is you visit the place where you will be interviewing the day before so you can see how the traffic is.

You can see exactly how far it is from your house or wherever you're coming from before the interview. You want to allow extra time to walk from your car to the desk, if you have to ride the elevator or walk the stairs you want to allow time for that, time to check in with the receptionist, because all this stuff takes time. You want to make sure that you're prompt for the interview.

Don't chew gum. This is a big mistake. You may find yourself sitting out in the lobby bored chewing gum. I have not seen anyone who looks good chewing gum, so don't chew gum. You could eat a peppermint if you need to before the interview, but you don't need to be chewing gum.

Always go prepared. I believe in wholeheartedly carrying a portfolio. You look so much more professional, and of course you want to take at least two extra resumes in case the potential employer wants a copy of your resume or has somebody there that wants a copy of your resume.

Before you go to the interview you want to make sure you look over the job description again and pull out those key skills that you have that you're currently using or that you've used in the past. Highlight them during the interview.

Take notes during the interview. You look more interested; you look more engaged. You look like you think this job is important.

Don't talk about salary, let the employer talk about salary first. Don't speak negatively about anyone, past employers, past employees, or coworkers, current coworkers or current employees. Don't speak negatively about anyone. Stay positive and upbeat during the interview.

Never, never, never wear jeans to an interview. Most of the time it's not even appropriate to wear clunky jewelry or clunky shoes, so just be careful with the shoes. You want to avoid loud perfumes, heels that are way too high. You got to be careful with colored hair. It could be offensive.

Negotiation

The next thing is negotiation. Ask for more than what you want. This I see a big, big problem in interviewing.

The thing is, you cannot ask for exactly how much money you want to make.

First of all, you should not be bringing this conversation up. Second of all if the employer asks you, you want them to offer whatever their offer is initially. But if you're pushed to where you have to say how much you want to make, you want to make sure that you ask for more than what you actually want.

Then the employer usually will come back and say yes or no. Or they might come back and say, "We can pay this." Then you can negotiate from there.

It's when you ask for exactly what you need that you will probably get something lower, because that's how negotiation works. The employer expects you to ask for more, then they're going to go a little higher, then you all will meet somewhere in the middle. You want to make sure you always ask for more.

Another thing, even though I have a master's in HR, I understand how the process works, I always believe in telling the employer that you make more than you actually do. The truth of the matter is; they have no way to determine if you really make what you say you make.

Of course within reason, you don't want to fudge it too much, but in order to grow substantially earning-wise, you have to tell the employer that you make more than what you make. You're usually not getting paid what your worth anyway.

Leave on good terms

Leave your current job on good terms. Always give a two weeks' notice, even if the new employer that wants to hire you wants you to be there in two days or a week.

Always give a two weeks' notice. What you have to think about is an employer who does not want you to give a two weeks' notice to a current employer may not be worth working for, but if you stand firm and say, "I have to give this employer a two weeks' notice." You will be respected so much more for that.

Be nice

Be nice to everyone from the person in the parking lot to the receptionist to the person that's interviewing you. The strangest thing happened to me. I went to interview years ago, and the lady at the front desk, I spoke to her, I was real nice.

She was talking to me, and I was just being nice, and it turns out that she was the CEO of the company. She just happened to be sitting at the front desk waiting on me for the interview. It was in the evening.

It was probably five o'clock, usually probably her time that she would normally leave. She was sitting at the front desk. You have to be careful how you treat people in the building, because you never know who the person is going to be the person that's going to interview you.

Networking

In *How to Win Friends and Influence People*, Dale Carnegie explains the "Six ways to make People like you

1. Become genuinely interested in other people.

2. Smile

3. Remember that a person's name is to that person the sweetest and most important sound in any language.

4. Be a good listener. Encourage others to talk about themselves.

5. Talk in terms of the other person's interests.

6. Make the other person feel important-and do it sincerely."

In The Little Black Book of Connections, author Jeffrey Gitomer explains, "The easiest way to compile a list of who you know is to create the list by group: friends, business friends, customers, coworkers, important people you may know casually, those on your Christmas card list, relatives, members from groups you belong to, and people you'd like to connect with. Once you've gathered your list of groups, call everyone you can and get their email addresses. Find out what their biggest needs are for this year, and begin to think of ways to communicate answers to those needs."

Jeffrey Gitomer goes on to say that "It's most likely that you have some form of contact database at the moment. But what you DON'T have is 1. A clear vision or definition of what these contacts mean to you or can do for you, and 2. A value-based game plan to connect and get what you want from them. There's a .5 One is what they mean to you, two is what they can do for you and 2.5 is what you can do for me. Guess which one is the most powerful, and guess which one is the least powerful. RULE ONE OF "THE MORE THE MORE": The more you do for them, the more they will do for you. The more you do for them, the more you will mean to them, and the more importance you will have in their lives. And of course, vice-versa."

Great networkers have a plan. They work to expand their network. Go the extra mile for people in your network. They know how to get the most value for their time. They communicate their messages effectively. Great networkers become experts.

They capture the best stories. They do what others don't do. People are drawn to them.

"Seek out those most successful around you and ask for help and guidance."

"Relationships are all there is. Everything in the universe only exist because it is in relationship to everything else. Nothing exists in isolation. We have to stop pretending we are individuals that can go it along." -Margaret Wheatley

Always work on building relationships. You want to build those relationships and go to networking events. Stay active in whatever your expertise is, or your niche is. You want to stay active in those associations. Whatever it is, you want to stay active in those associations so you can build relationships.

You want to have some kind of a plan of action of how you're going to get a job, so say for example if you have one company in mind, it's always good to have several companies in mind that you're targeting, trying to get a job with.

You can usually look up on LinkedIn or even Google, or look up the company's website and see who the hiring managers are, who the supervisors are for their area, and you can kind of target companies that way. I always believe in, whatever job you're looking for, you want to target the manager over that particular ... That manager's manager.

If you're looking for a job, your perfect job, you want to plan to commit twenty to thirty hours a week to your job search. You can expect to submit two hundred to three hundred resumes. This is not short-term.

This takes work if you want to get the job that you really want. Pay attention to the numbers. For example, if you submit three hundred resumes and you get four interviews, you want to pay attention to the ratio: resumes to interviews. Work to improve those ratios.

Does it take two hundred resumes to get one interview? Does it take three hundred resumes to get one interview? If you find that you have to do three hundred resumes to get one interview, you want to make sure that you're doing the keyword targeting. Not necessarily just submitting resumes from your phone.

You want to make sure you take the time to tailor that resume to what the potential employer is asking you for. What requirements are they asking you for?

Also you want to look at the job requirements as a whole. What qualifications do you really have? What do they ask for that you don't have? Is there something that you can do to get those qualifications, to earn those skills, to learn those skills? If you see that you don't have the qualifications or you're way off, you want to try to do an informational interview. Basically you can call up the company, you can call HR or you can call that particular supervisor or manager over that department, you could ask for a informational interview. Basically the informational interview, the first one is to build a relationship with that particular manager/supervisor, and two, you want to find out their path, how did they get to that particular job? Three, you want to see what you have to do to be hired. How could you get a job? What qualifications are required?

Even though some of this stuff you could find out on your own, you want to put your name out there in front of that particular manager or supervisor. You want to find out what they did, and this will help you on your path. Maybe you won't get hired from that company, but you will learn a lot about what companies look for that particular job or that position.

In order to get the job that you want you really have to become a better employee where you currently are. You want to make sure that you're working hard, that you're there before you're supposed to be there, or at least on time. Make sure that you're staying all day, and then a little bit later. You want to make sure that you're working the whole time that you're working, and that you're going the extra mile.

That you're not just coming to work and then only working fifteen minutes the whole day or two hours the whole day. You want to make sure that if you're being paid to work eight hours that you're working eight hours. If you're surfing the internet all day long you want to make sure that you stop surfing the internet and get to work. You want to work all the time that you're working.

Join Associations in your Field

Become a joiner in your area or your niche or specialty. Join associations in your niche. You want to find out who's who, you want to find out who the hiring managers are, what companies they work for.

Read one hour a day in your area of expertise, this will help you dramatically move ahead to get the job that you want. You will learn so much about your particular area of expertise. You will certainly learn a lot more than the people that are currently working in your field, because most people aren't reading. This could be books, journals, articles, blogs by thought leaders.

Create and complete a profile for the top big Job sites which include Careerbuilder, Indeed, Job.com, The Ladders, SimplyHired and Monster.

You might consider creating your own website. For example, www.yourname.com, so for me it would be www.shondamiles.com. Put your resume and cover letter on that website. If you write articles you could put your articles on their pertaining to your expertise. If you want you can list the association that you're a member of, you could put a link to your social media profile, like your LinkedIn profile. You want to make sure that you have a complete LinkedIn profile. Try to get recommendations on your profile. Be sure that you've completed the employment part of the profile. Go through each section and make sure each section is completed. Make sure that you add those keywords in that's indicative of your particular expertise. Make a list of your accomplishments. You need to know all of your accomplishments that you've achieved, as well as your strengths. If you've had good reviews, you want to have a list of those as well.

Take responsibility

I take responsibility. Say it with me. I don't blame anyone for my situation. If you don't have the job you want, consider the following:

1. What 5 skills do you need for the job you want? Do you have them?

2. Do you do things with a smile? Can your supervisor and coworkers depend on you?

3. Do you need to improve the skills? Are you constantly improving them?

4. Are you clear on exactly what that job is and how to go about getting it? Do you know the qualifications? Do you have the qualifications?

5. Do you send a tailored resume and cover letter for every job you apply to?

6. Are you spending 20 hours a week looking for a job? Looking for a job is a full time job.

7. Can you ask for a raise? Do you deserve a raise? Can you prove it? Do you have a list of your accomplishments measureable outcome?

8. Are you working all the time you are at work?

9. Are you always on time? Or do you cost the company money?

10. Are you prepared for work? Are you organized?

11. Are you positive? Do you have a positive attitude?

12. Do you know who the top people are that are in your field? Make a list. Create a plan to build a relationship with them. What associations are they apart of? If you want to get the job you want, you have to prepare yourself to do a lot of things you haven't done already.

13. Do you go the extra mile?

14. Do you come to work early?

15. Do you stay late?

16. Do you prepare at least 1 hour before every interview?

17. Have you asked your supervisor for feedback?

18. Do you always miss work?

19. Are you sloppy?

20. Are you lazy?

21. Are you the gossip at work?

Develop a Plan. "If you are failing to plan, you are failing to plan." A plan is essential for growth. Start with a list of things you need to do to find a job and improve your skills. Add to it as you come across more things that need to be done. "Create a definite plan for carrying out your desire, and begin at once, whether you're ready or not, to put it into action." -- Napoleon Hill

Take the most important Goal and write it down. Create a plan to achieve it.

What strategies you will use to accomplish them?

About the Author

Shonda Miles has been self-employed for 18 years. She has owned businesses ranging from an online retail store to a Training Company.

Shonda Miles is the CEO of Shonda Miles International, a company helping organizations and individuals improve performance and achieve their goals. Shonda Miles is here to help you achieve your full potential. Her purpose is to help millions of people achieve their goals and live their God given talent.

Shonda Miles is an Author, Entrepreneur, Speaker, Personal Development Trainer, Business Consultant and Business Coach. She loves reading Nonfiction books, writing business books and shopping. Personal Development is her mission. Shonda speaks, blogs and writes about a variety of personal development topics such as Time Management, Success, Goal Setting and having a Positive Attitude.

Shonda's goal is to help others achieve the level of success they desire.

Shonda Miles is a MBA Graduate. She has several successful businesses.

Shonda Miles can be reached at info@shondamiles.com or via her website at www.shondamiles.com.

www.ingramcontent.com/pod-product-compliance
Lightning Source LLC
Chambersburg PA
CBHW070337190526
45169CB00005B/1937

* 9 7 8 1 5 3 2 7 2 7 4 8 1 *